Also by John Rybicki

We Bed Down into Water

Traveling at High Speeds

by Julie Moulds

The Woman with a Cubed Head

When All the World Is Old

When All the World Is Old

poems

JOHN RYBICKI

LOOKOUT BOOKS
University of North Carolina Wilmington

First printing, April 2012
ISBN: 978-0-9845922-6-5

Cover photograph ©Irene Suchocki
Book design by Arianne Beros, Meg Reid, and Anna Sutton
for The Publishing Laboratory

LIBRARY OF CONGRESS CATALOGING-IN-PUBLICATION DATA

Rybicki, John, 1961–
When all the world is old : poems / John Rybicki.
    p. cm.
ISBN 978-0-9845922-6-5 (alk. paper)
I. Title.
PS3568.Y3977W44 2012
811'.54—dc23
                                        2011052287

ART WORKS.
arts.gov

Lookout Books gratefully acknowledges support from the University of North Carolina Wilmington and the National Endowment for the Arts.

Lookout Books
Department of Creative Writing
University of North Carolina Wilmington
601 S. College Road
Wilmington, NC 28403
www.lookout.org

For the nurses,
tender warriors all,
and for Julie

Contents

When All the World Is Old

When all the world is old, lad,
    And all the trees are brown;
And all the sport is stale, lad,
    And all the wheels run down;
Creep home, and take your place there,
    The spent and maimed among:
God grant you find one face there,
    You loved when all was young.

— Charles Kingsley

What power had I
Before I learned to yield?
Shatter me, great wind:
I shall possess the field.

— Richard Wilbur

I

*When you are in danger, the adrenaline quickens; your senses are heightened.
You realize, I am not dead yet, but I could be soon. And each day means
more than it ever has. You're on the edge of the canyons fighting the winds.
The cancer has tried to get me, but it has not gotten me yet. I am singing and
building walls against it: not me not me not me . . .*

One Body

This is her last night out in the world.
The gray sky's tossing down its crumbs

and it's getting dark. "You're so good to me,"
she says, gazing across this bridge of light

we make every time we look at each other.
The light is threadlike, but you can trust it,

you can hold on to it. "You're crazy," I say.
"What, you want me to smash this ice-cream cone

against my forehead to prove it?" And I do.
We crush our way through what is left

and kiss each other's fingers. My Dame and I,
we linger for hours like this,

cracking our pens together like swords.
One body, really, like you dream about.

One Wish

If love could grant one wish
it would be this: I would bloom
and take Julie inside me, keep her
safe, leave one lantern rocking
in the night sky over her head,
where God's heart should be.

My Dame and I in the Twenty-Dollar Cancer Room

Julie puts on her bedtime silk so we can be close.
She can barely keep her eyes open after a hard week
of visiting family and friends. She's straining
to do just that—stay awake and make it last.

I stroke her arm up under the silk, trace my fingers
around the chemo port on the heart side of her chest—
that bump like a little box of matches tucked under the skin.
I remember pacing outside the hospital room

when they installed it, a palace guard on his watch,
a protector of one. Every inch of her skin shines
under this touching. She's almost smiling in her sleep,
though her eyes are bruised from so much chemo.

It looks like some dark elf has been hammering
her with his fists directly over each of her eyes.
In the morning I'll surrender her to all those white arms,
step with her into the belly of the whale.

With Julie's satin top spread open above her breasts,
the flaps on the collar are the pearl wings of a bird.
Her sternum's the spine for this bird with its wings
spread across her chest. I'll have to tell her about it

come morning. I watch my love sleep and write while I watch.
There's a wind love makes out of us: my Dame's alive
in the world and she's breathing, or love is breathing
through her—through her mouth and through her skin.

She has hollered "I love you, Dude" from our porch
as I fling one arm out the window and drive away.
That wind still travels the earth. Beyond the lamp shade
and her silk, the shag carpet littered with empty bottles

and notebooks; beyond the market just over the border
of Zion where you can buy beer along with your fish;
beyond concrete and tar miles with all those metal bees
buzzing over roads...there is so vast an earth and sky.

I tell you my wife is the center of it all. Everything grows
from her. Julie lies in her bedtime silk, this little bird puffing
in her throat. There's the white whale outside our motel window
and I'm wrapping my arms around every second.

Sleep now, my cruel one, sleep.
Your Dude is on his watch.

Notice Me

A pigtailed girl bounces
away from the ice-cream shop with her double
    chocolate scoops topped

with chocolate sprinkles.
She notices Julie's bald head shining from beneath
    the African hat she's wearing.

All the light in the girl skids
along the concrete, stops—mid-lick, mid-stride—
    so her very skin seems to be gazing

over at my lass. Julie's snug
under the loop of my arm, pressing her whole self,
    cell upon cell, through my side.

I'm trying to smuggle her
out of a burning city. Whatever you do,
    love, don't look back.

I want to carry her inside me,
a double-dose Johnny, a pregnant man on the street
    with this lovely bushel

of apple blossoms beneath
his skin. My gal does not peel away when I
    reach for the door and open it.

She does not tear out of me
when I can't quite fit us both through the opening.
    "Keep me safe," she says.

I Straddle the Earth

I straddle the earth reaching far-flung ends of the compass,
    tugging red and yellow and orange thread
out of living things, weaving them about my love's wrists.
    I can see her shadowy limbs

through the light-colored skirt, the sun tossing down beams
    in collusion with the eyes, igniting those timepiece
legs swinging. Then the subtle ticktock as she walks away.
    She's making these walls my hiding place,

tearing bread from under her blouse until there is no flesh
    and I disappear behind her shirt, which she pins
on the line in our yard. Tumors galore in my love's neck
    and what with her tapered haircut,

I see them all. The things I say holding her while the oaks
    let fly in leaf spray their alphabets, and wind whips
upon that larger page. I snap my hands at invisible things:
    all those leftover particles from that first explosion

when God so loved his own body he blew it up and gave us
    boxes to haul around kissing the germs inside.
Sometimes we don't see our body for what it is: atoms,
    molten dancer feet vibrating over our muscle and bone.

When I roll over near my love under the covers
    the taste is singular, a wave crash that is body heat.
I want to bake my love solid in this casket, or mandate
    two bone boxes with holes bored through their sides

so close our hands are touching. Out into clay they clasp
    and melt around each other. I'd even wish our bones
in one box, but who on top of whom? My weight on top of hers?
    To have her bear that weight through all eternity?

Yes, I'd do it, or my weight under hers. I'd like that better.
   Her face on my chest peaceful as in life.
Even our skeletons are in love, she says, my Old World Dame
   who was not born: she sensed I needed her,

slipped down from some seventeenth-century painting,
   and started off across the earth to find me. At night
the bees inside my love finally quiet, though they swarm
   my mouth when we kiss and kiss.

The ricochet of those beautiful bullets in my caverns.
   All afternoon I'm a storm on two feet
preaching to empty pews. When I'm done I buzz
   in my metal wagon back to our cave, find her

on a knoll of burnt prairie grass, all her face an ache.
   No, I missed it. When she first spread her
butterfly arms upon that hill, I thought, My God,
   we both know it: she's already dead.

So we eat each other alive. Mornings we haul out bees
   in boxes with red ribbon bows,
and chase the paperboy leaving them on porches.
   I am the rattle she shakes back at heaven,

and when we kiss she holds my mouth hostage,
   the queen bee buzzing under her tongue.

Why Everything Is a Poem

There's my ashen girl in the stands
with a scarf over her soft to steel-wool head.
She's there like some buoy next to a friend
she calls sister, who has been riding
a separate current now for years.

It has been too much for too long and we know it
is time to take hold of the lightning and let it kill her,
or fill her—doctor or angel or nurse—
like some new balloon and set her glancing
across the rooftops with her dancing slippers.

She'll sprinkle a little sand over each roof
and soft-shoe it for the sleepers.
I can't hide the hawks. I can't hide the crows
under my tongue and tell my lass so
kneeling beside her in the bathroom.

Can I learn to love the ashes of this world,
turn my palms to the sky like the first snow
is sifting down? Can I catch my love on my tongue
after she is gone, close my eyes while my own wife
dissolves into me? We're on a possible farewell tour

visiting old friends when she tilts her face
my way from the stands. We make in one look
a hammock of our blood and I pool where she pools,
drink from that well of loneliness in her
I can't quite loop my arms around.

Then we turn again to where our friend's son
skates gladiatorial with his long hair fluttering
from beneath his hockey helmet.
That boy who once swam across my belly
reaching to pinch my bristly chin hairs.

I sing to keep the embers in the night sky alive—
those sparks God tows out of my love's chest
each night. I sing from the crown of her stubbled head
to the arch of her foot where I'd kiss and kiss her
till she said, Dude, rub in the love like you do.

I sing her dripping just out of the bathtub,
her finger squeaking against the steam
on the bathroom window where she's scrawling
her last love note to my own son and me. She's singing
the words over and over as she writes, *I love my boys,*

leaning hard on the *o* in *love.*
She leaves a heart and words that reappear
when we place our mouths close to the glass.
My son and I fog it with our breath
after she is gone.

Mud That Shelves Adam's Ribs

God, petrify my heart. I cannot
take up arms like the grass does
and march in legions of myself,
cannot wrap myself like wool
around a baby's crib.

No wonder mothers sew
with any kind of fabric
that which might replicate
the walls of their own flesh.
Fathers prowl with fangs
along the blue slats of this pen
where a daughter moves
like a rose bitten off at the stem.

Mothers spend their lives stitching
soft clothing. I make paper
and cover it with music. I cannot
sew the paper into a fabric
to cover, say, the hospital bed
where my love burns in the cancer
skillet and is no more.

The embryo stars keep wiggling.
The children on my street ring
like bells inside their clothes.
They load water balloons under their shirts
then smash them, frolic in puddles
laughing and chasing after an ant
floating along the curb on a twig.

Why do I have all this piss
folded into the jewel in my chest
when the next and next girl or boy
do nothing but hump and make dew?

What lifeboat do I shape
around even an acorn inside
those children when I spread
my preacher arms in some ghetto school
trying to drag a marching drummer
out of each student's chest?

The train whistle might be whistling
from east to west in each of our chests.
The sky might still be a great blue
and moody balloon. Some nights
caskets might slide like bumper cars
colliding in the earth.

Why can't I say yes to the laughter in my chest?

As a boy I went door to door with the sun
turning to crushed coals. I gathered everyone
and we stood on our lawns in our pajamas.
We waved good night to one another
latching hold of the sidewalks,
which we opened like drawers
and climbed inside to sleep.

Tender Range

Come the white morning
I'll cross the earth on my face.

Let the barrel of light tip over
one more time and let's call it sunrise.

I don't know anything about
blowing a child out like a balloon,

or what comes after—that dream like a waterfall
sealed in a flask close to God's hip.

It's night now with those squares
of light all over the world,

there where a woman has been
spreading her own light onto the windows

of her house just like I have
rubbed oil onto my love's belly.

Mothers daub their own fire to the glass
so even a scarecrow like me

out wandering the night
can take his chin from inside his coat,

there where his own lantern is hissing,
to gaze through the glass and stop

the crunch of footfalls over the bones
of things I cannot fix. Do you know

how many hobos like me are out there
where the wind howls? We gaze up from where

her fire pours over the snow: because we know
she is in there doing her soft work.

Near the Old Packard Plant

An old man comes trolling
potbellied past the factory

with its burnt yellow grass.
He's pedaling his molecules

jumpity and in mourning,
the windup key in his back.

The sun's a counterfeit round
and should be shaped like a sickle

as God is a great head clopper.
Bless this beautiful brother

shining out of nowhere
and trolling in the center ring

where the whip cracks
over his head, and the circus

strongman blows a bubble
so big and round we call it the sky.

We're in Church the Day Before Her Bone Marrow Transplant

when Julie wraps her arms around her own chest
to crush away the fear. Keep me safe, she says,

and I throw my arms around as much of her as I can hold.
We kneel before Mass and pray with our faces

bowed and knees kissing. We hold that pose a long while.
When she lifts her head Julie's straw hat tumbles

into the pew in front of us. There's a wiggler down there,
boy three or four crawling along behind his parents.

Julie's hat has flopped like some treasure right before
his blue eyes and he pinches it in his fingers.

The boy's father is a tower over his prayer book
turning from the altar to the boy now lifting

the hat to where Julie and I take it from him like some gift
and press it back into place on Julie's head.

Her face shines from under her gypsy white scarf
and I shine with her.

Dancing with My Lass to Elvis Costello

First night alone in the new apartment.
The spirits draw up from the hard things
of this world. The oak floor and trim,
even the walls warm to malleable,

wrap themselves like a shawl around my animal.
I put on some Elvis Costello and shape my arms
to hold Julie's form, as if she were there
in the hollow under my chin. Is it Elvis

or some acoustic angel sprinkling my love's
spirit near her man, who leans his pillars
from foot to foot, his palm gripping no more
than the apparition of her baby-bald head?

×

They say that grief is a tidal wave
and when it hits it staggers me
to the living room floor. I kneel
and hold my hand to the distance
the way my love did every time

she'd chalk away over the stones
in our driveway, turn signal winking
left so the squirrels and such would know
which way she was going. She'd curl
onto the blacktop and squeal the brakes,

jut her arm out the car window, her hand
straining to drag the arm almost out
by its socket and fly her back to me.
Were those bracelets, or little bells
of cancer jingling along her arm?

×

My lass and I were citizens of that magnification.
We were blood tulips. Wreaths laced with ribbons
circled each of our throats as I stood there in my socks
on our cement slab porch, replicating the gesture,

willing my arm to tear out by its root and chase
after her. Julie would ease off the brakes at the apex
of our little world and let gravity take her.
She'd surrender downhill to that river sweeping

her toward her own death. Sometimes I'd cry
or she'd cry around the bend to the elements,
"I love you, Dude, I love you, Dude," her voice
always softer the second time with distance.

Julie the Valiant

I leave the library and find where my jumping bean
    terrier has shattered the glass
over our bicycle-built-for-two wedding photo.

I could drain a billion silkworms of their thread
    writing about that photo:
loved ones sprinting after us with their cameras

snapping as I went jockey up in the stirrups,
    pumping my legs to launch us
across the grass. Julie with her legs wide behind me

so her pedals spun freely. We're posing on that hillside
    afterward, with the "Just Married" signs
painted on cardboard and hanging from each set of handlebars.

The sun's gone but still a blinding sheet of rose behind us.
    My lass in her vintage wedding
dress leans her whole self against my back,

joy lighting her face even though she seems at repose.
    I'm not smiling in the photo
the way Julie is: I've absorbed the awful rays

of my parents' marriage and cancelled two weddings;
    I've slung my demons like hanged men
over the cornfield, and in my face only fierceness and resolve.

✖

My Julie the Valiant used to say so many times,
    leaving to go somewhere
and in an almost panic, "I wish I had a little version of you,

a little Johnny I could take along in my pocket to keep me safe."
    Then she'd take that little Johnny
out of her pants pocket and pet him on his head.

She'd scrunch up her face like a four-year-old
    clenching that Johnny
to her heart and hugging the little doll.

My lass swaggered like a prizefighter down the alleys
    of cancer, yet got so shivery
vulnerable anytime she had to leave the house.

I'd brace myself when she came charging, a little Italian
    freight train bursting into my arms.
She'd crush the breath right out of me. We all try

to armor up, weather and walk this earth, curtsy and smile,
    make light happen through our faces
as we talk and talk, but it takes this spiritual exertion.

If you are lucky you'll find one choice soul who becomes
    your safe ground. They'll gather
your war shield and say, "No, I will carry this for you.

I will go before you and lead the way." You must believe
    the wounds in your love to be exquisite.
No other woman but Julie stood up to the storm that is me.

Some drank, even in lavish doses, the constellations
    and aliveness that moved through me.
She was the only one who ever threw her arms around the hurricane

and did not let go. I guess I made for her that safe place
    where she could surrender,
let a whole forest of trees fall down inside her, fall down in my arms,

if that's what she needed to do. Did I keep you safe, Curd?
    Did I keep you safe?
What was looming, forever looming, has come to pass.

You died, my sweet Curd. The winter wind chimes crash
    against our house, and the light of love
is on, and you're never coming home ever again.

                              ✼

I test our Boo-Dawg to see if he remembers you.
    Even after six months
when I say, "Is it Mom? Is that Mom coming home?"

his brown fur goes electric near the living room window,
    ears cocked as he eyes the street
to see if it is you. I will dunk these sounds and syllables

in holy water. I will let pour from my nostrils in flame,
    stand in defiance
of our parting and go to war to make you live again.

I can see you sashaying in your old dancing skirt,
    lifting it above those anklets
you wore like some bobby-soxer from the fifties.

You're twirling near the window of our old apartment,
    there by the light of one candle.
You're tap dancing in the high country now with Fred and Ginger,

aren't you, Dame? Are those stars the bits of steel
        you have fastened to the bottoms
of your tap shoes? Are you twirling solo

with your arms shaped to fit around the bones of your Johnny,
        even though I'm still marooned
in this world? Have you seen me dancing with you in our empty house

when our son is gone, our dogs scrabbling around
        my feet like it's some kind of game?
I am a staggerer now, love, not a dancer.

I stagger around in these blood boots that moor me
        to the earth. One day
I'll pack your vintage wedding dress

and my vintage suit, load them into the kind of luggage
        we can lift clean into the air.
Don't love any other dance partner you might find

in the sky too much, okay? Dame of my heart,
        if this page is a kind of earth,
then I'm watering this earth with my tears.

II

People have been raining presents down on me all week: hats, beads, good luck stones, cancer stones, precious stones, lending me money. I can feel this vault swing open inside them, can feel their light flooding into the hidden places in me until I am less frightened. I want to love my Dude until we're old.

We Dance on a Spinning Log

that spins too fast
and then we get erased.
The red and yellow leaves

tickle at first, then burn
all the way down our throats
when they fall.

Who will grease our arms
for the ones we love?
We release them

to white bedsheets first,
then to a blanket made of earth.
They slip through no matter

how much we hoard
their ruby fire and wind.
How curious to see

the empty lantern
inside the casket
no longer hissing,

to feel my phantom spirit
tear through flesh and hurl itself
into her arms to sleep the last sleep

with her after so many nights
in the tropics. What if
we snapped and did it,

hurled ourselves into the casket
chasing after that flare of spirit
that's already made the leap?

Who would drag us back
into the open air to dig our claws
into the blue curtain of this world?

✖

See here this endless drip,
these drops of fire
that fell from the heavens

and lodged in each of us.
Some mornings we wake to find
at the ends of our wrists

paintbrushes instead of fingers.
We rise with the sky father to paint
and to kiss each rooftop good morning.

Sweet joy with all of these
shattered feathers
in our mouths.

We hover over our dead,
knock softly at that door,
or bang our fists at the earth,

this to ignite the heart
that once tapped its foot in time
to the music in our chests.

We make behind our ribs
a kind of church where
the candles burn like children

in a fallout shelter. What we say
to the snapping wind is this:
Even you aren't allowed in here.

And we bundle those children
under our coats
like any mother would.

I'm Old Enough to Be My Own Father

I crest the hillside with my coffee mug
and leash in hand, wishing for a dogsled
behind the Jack Russell we call Sparky.

He claws across the blacktop
spooling out of me so much thread.
This from the dim wick of the spine

where it unravels. The cries from two
children tambourine the lake, and I drink
that alien thing, innocence.

It's not quite fall. The trees are still
such symphonies of green, not so ashen
when I sneeze and blow them all away.

                    ✳

I marveled, as an altar boy rising before the sun
was baking its bread, what on earth
could will those ragtag souls out of bed

morning after morning, their faces bowed
along the pews like wanted men.
They seemed folded with their overcoats

in darkness. I marveled in my bright freckles
and smock over what reverence or woe
tugged them like sheep to where the sun

came washing through the stained-glass bodies
of Moses and Jesus and Mary.
They crawled out of that womb of sleep

by choice and amassed themselves
under their heavy clothes.
They migrated toward the altar

to lay their secrets at the feet
of the two-story Christ
hanging on the cross behind me.

✳

I'd feel the weariness of the sleeping bear
in the priest called to rise and preach and drink
the wine with that new light spilling over the pews.

I'd shake the branches of heaven behind the altar,
jingle the bells way up over our heads.
I felt so lucky to be on my knees

with my palms pressed together under my throat.
And I spied on them. Every morning I tunneled
behind the altar to where my vestments hung.

I donned that altar boy smock like a thing
that had been brushed by angels.
I carried the cross to the altar with their eyes

all over me, the sting of bees stuffed down in my cheeks.
I wanted so desperately to laugh. During Communion
all those tongues came falling out from inside the trap.

I'd follow beside the priest and slide
the paten under their chins so no scrap
of Christ's flesh could fall to the floor.

The church sat so light on my shoulders after Mass.
There was no forlorn clown with a broom
sweeping those parishioners toward the exits.

The congregation adjourned to the separate rivers
that swept their lives until St. Clare of Montefalco
became a hollowed-out thing.

Sometimes the priest, even at that hour in the back room
of that tavern, would drain every last drop of the living
blood of Christ, and believe me I was tempted.

✻

Remember, this is a poem about walking
your shadows with your light and your dog
and what you relish along the way.

I wonder what rivers rush or return inside you,
and how might you lift them like living thread
to sew into the clothing of those you love.

There's a Riptide of Human Stars

More and more I can't
be captive to this velocity,
    held hostage by the flesh
and torque of this earth.

    Sometimes I grind my heels
against space, say no to this
    volition, close my eyes and
just spend time with the dead.

    They bloom through the veil of sleep,
rocking their ancient lanterns.
    My gut wiring won't change:
I stuff the fields under my coat,

    shove the whisk broom wisps of light
back over the mountaintops,
    there where the ghosts tow their bright
linen across the firmament.

    I can't keep pace with
the jack-in-the-box students
    popping up through the floorboards
and flaring their arms at me.

    A mountain is something solid
to hold in the chest. I study it like
    a corollary to man, while my godson
C.J. scrabbles his feet

    over the word scraps littering
the floor. There's a plank
    across the sky he's dancing on,
his feet in their wildness.

Some belowdecks timekeeper slams
a red mallet against my godson's ribs
        and he starbursts into my arms.
He shreds my pajama bottoms

        after I thump him in a game of marbles.
I tell him I am the whodunnit master of all
        marble players. His laughter chugs a train
up a hill so steep even Christ

        in his steel slippers couldn't climb it.
C.J. breaks down the bathroom door
        when I call the girl back East. Boy or no,
I tell him, she's a fireproof blanket

        draped over my shoulders. He falls down
to sleep next to me. I wake in the middle
        of the night stroking my Sparky dog's head
seven or eight times before I realize it's C.J.

        In the morning, after push-ups
and pillow fights and coffee,
        we ridge about in our hiking boots,
slide down the snowy slopes into gullies.

        We slip our fingers into the hoof tracks
of elk to taste a little of their wildness.
        We ghost about the teeth of wolves,
and when sunlight bathes the dead

        or dying scrub grass, we bend
to the earth to gather
        fistfuls of those oats
flaming inside a human mouth.

Our Dead Float Under Us

The chessboard is circular,
but some moves matter more than others.
     We plant our feet there,

     gaze under the horse's chin
to where each stalk of corn blazes.
     Those underground altar boys

     and girls inch up through soil,
raise the swords they once carried to the altar.
     Not to maim but to offer heaven

     those flames that live on inside us.
Every night our dead float under us.
     They kiss away at the floorboards,

     offer a bouquet of ash
through a rib cage that has fallen away
     soft as snow.

     One day you find your face
in a window just waiting for the sunlight
     to pour in. If you are lucky,

     another house slides along the landscape,
and a woman inside lifts her chin over the windowsill
     at the same moment you do.

     Let her trembling lip be the prayer
that builds the new world.
     Let the silk that spills between you

     knit itself together in the air.
For the sun is a heavy egg on its journey,
     and who knows what weary traveler

might need a bed like yours,
a place where even one of his feathers
can fall and rest.

I Reach Through the Cobwebs, Ice, and Weariness

I wish I didn't have to piss in the middle of the night,
climb from that warm pool where I unknit my life story.
My mister gray chin, Boo-Dawg, paws his way behind me,
jingles his dog tags near the sofa right where my son is sleeping.
He clatters to where I turn the doorknob three or four times—
safecracker style—in case there's a skunk grazing in our yard.

In the morning my son scratches my bedroom door,
gives it a thump to wake me up. I coo bright sounds like
"Okay, my man," wince, and try to whip myself onto my feet.
You have to go on for the boy.

I rise and scrub my teeth, gravel some chow into the dog dish.
Then run away from my haunted house, the things in our nest
that are hers: homemade watermelon or vanilla-cinnamon
or cocoa butter lip balms; homemade soaps shaped like moons
and stars; lavender or citrus spray bottles she'd mist into the air,
then bid Martell or me to step into that fine rain of scent
and just breathe. I run away from her Virgin Mary pictures
and prayer cards taped to our windows, regal Mary statues
resting on our counters; Mary nailed and hung on the wall.

I drop Martell off at school and take my monastery
to Bowen's Diner. Most mornings my singular wish is this:
Someone please light a smile when I enter and nod,
place me somewhere in the world.

Today I took my turn in the bathroom after Martell and his
shower and steam. I didn't just do the toothpaste and rinse,
then kneel to wash my hair in the deepening rust of the tub.
I didn't just tether my dogs to one leash and out the door
cajoling them into flight. "Get 'em, Booger. Get 'em, Sparky."
Sparky rips across the grass on his cigar legs, nipping Boo
on the ass, Boo fishtailing on his rump to swing around and
jab his snout under Sparky's belly, flip him right over in the air.

It is beautiful but it is work. Like eating is work.

I set my hounds free, then bait them back with a hot dog or honk
on my horn, load them into our hut for an all-day lockdown.
Yes, Dame, water in the dish, too.

On this particular morning I pick one of her things
to take with me, or it picks me: I reach through the cobwebs,
ice, and weariness, lift her little box of wristwatch bands.
She has red and rust and green and black bands—nine in all—
strung along a Styrofoam wrist. Her wrist. All those decorative
bands she'd match up with her outfits.

There's the red band at the end of the line with the watch itself
still keeping perfect time along her arm after she is gone.

Night and Its Strange Likeness to a Diego Rivera Mural

I shadowbox the sheet hanging over the opening
to the back of my house,
tacked up to trap in the heat.

I jab sometimes with knives in each hand
shredding the sheet before me,
or with a hammer-like swing

to the right stab at the bathroom door.
At my gym a young Mexican man
beams and asks if I'm training for a fight.

No, just fighting my own *demonios*.
He laughs but nods his head to this.
Tonight I'm just fists against the wall.

Most nights I prop my mattress
against the wall, then switch
to fighting southpaw, an alien feel.

I'm a soldier training for no war
in an age where the menace is a field in the brain:
I'm snapping kicks at my refrigerator

to pass the nights in this ghost house.
Even bow hunting with the rain
of yellow and red leaves

that fall like hands all around me,
I wonder has nature finally placed my heart on its anvil
and hammered what my father tried to provide

when he slapped the scars onto my skin like medals.
Armor up, boy. The sun may as well
have brass knuckles at the ends of its beams.

Tire Shop Poem

I grunt at the tire shop. I bottom-dweller fish
    so others can float around on my outstretched palm.
I lay mine tar smashed in my love's lap, on her milky wrist.
    The hand as relic with its swirl of furrows no one is plowing.

I am William Blake's brother. I'm doing penance
    after so high-wire an act—the pet bird on God's ring finger.
I puddle down in slop to hoist and hubcap,
    wa-zing zing lug nuts on and off.

Then over to the Rim Clamp where I sluice a full moon
    of lubricant around each bead, clock- then counterclockwise,
spin and popcorn pop rubber onto rims. I foot-petal punch
    to unclamp the wheel, then roll the bouncing brick

to where Dalton smacks lead earrings on the wheel
    until the balancer rolls out zeros in the fallen world.
It's early. We're drinking coffee, relearning our bodies
    and what we do with them:

we're flicking lighters, pinching the trigger on the impact gun,
    or finding things like Styrofoam cups or trays
from yesterday's takeout. I kept my lid open for the mice.
    These bits of ourselves we left on purpose

to prove the next day we were really there.
    We gather these traces and get swept
away from that animal that once wore our skin.
    Maybe we're ready to be done with him,

another self to toss in the Dumpster,
    another self that earned his nightly pleasure boat.
We hit the time clock and this new river snatches ahold of us.
    We ride our molecules to the coffeepot,

make our dull geometry from wire wheel brush
        to socket set, to watercooler.
When the pony kicks in our chests, we lunge forward,
        ride out the momentum from each blast.

There's Dalton on his hands and knees jacking a car up.
        Corey pries the hubcaps off like scabs,
and the compressor hums and clicks.
        Sean rolls four new Cooper Cobras in and we get busy

in our orchestra pit. We're snapping off old valve stems
        that gush with all that breath let loose from the bottle.
We're in this pit, a pit crew racing the light as it enters our cave
        breaking the same wheel on the same damn clock.

I sweep its crumbs up with the old valve stems.
        I bundle Carrie's suicide notes as she drags on a smoke.
She says, Thanks, Dogger, as I heave away from the hoist
        the latest rust bucket we've laid hands on.

Carrie climbs in, her body slender as a candle
        an altar boy might carry along the interstate
where her newly ex-husband's out trolling in his semi
        going nowhere like the rest of us.

We lose track counting her arms that fell off,
        enough arms or wings to fill boxcars with.
You could count those boxcars passing all day
        with your soda pop or beer

and still not get to the end of your counting.
        We bundle those arms that snap off of her,
though they grow back each day
        swinging like ropes at her side.

Now Dalton's flicking a few matchsticks on the floor
    and waiting for Carrie to drive her seven thousand
and eighty-fifth car into the first bay.
    We lean like beehives near the window

where she swirls one finger near her ear, as if to say,
    Bartender, the drinks are on me, only it's four tires, boys.
We kneel in night puddle water and cigarette butts
    to find the car's bones and jack it up, make one thing

in this sore world float on air for awhile,
    just cool up there breezy with all the angels.
Sometimes Carrie climbs the steel staircase to the terrace
    where we stack aluminum and old metal rims,

boxes filled with tubes for fixing flat tires.
    She's on the steps smoking and hovering. Dalton and I have her
between two Rim Clamps like two birdbaths spinning
    when Dalton steps on the gas and punches her soft

in the side of the face with a nice airburst.
    Her hair whooshes up and she laughs an ashen laugh,
then stone shoves the softness from her face.
    Come midmorning there's a lull in the thunder cave:

Dalton cups his hands to Corey's ear and they slip out,
    climb into the semi where we lace runaway and geriatric tires,
where steel belts can gash open even a rough hand.
    They're passing a joint with their butts planted

in a nice lounge chair of rubber. Corey laughs like a trumpet blast
    when I roll the dolly past—Dogger, you want a taste?
I say no thanks to that perfume, listen later to his puffed cheeks
    telling me not enough gas money to go see his kids.

I'm kicking my own empty pockets while we sunbathe
      in that spotlight where Fred Astaire might be dancing,
though that won't buy him a tank of gas. Dalton's way back there
      in the semi laughing through his beard and tar bib.

He's one of those walking tattoos.
      He has a monster on each forearm
dropping a thick and gooey spiderweb from its fingers;
      then there's a heart with some blurry initials in it,

a woman's face he sketched when he was locked up
      on assault charges drawing and daubing the blood away.
You'd have to lean your ladder against the moon
      then climb way up it to clock him in the face.

Dalton likes to sneak up behind me when I'm face-bowed
      to some wheel, T-shirt over my nose like some bandit
grinding a cloud of corrosion off with my wire wheel brush.
      He electrocutes me with two soft fingers in the ribs,

his teeth a little yellow around the edges. He can drink a thirty-pack
      in one night and not get smashed;
has a mom with a little blue rattler pickup truck
      that has a sticker in the rear window that reads,

My Son was Convict of the Month at the County Jail.
      May your bones shine like mine do, lucky as I am to know
these rubber-slinging virtuosos, these cavemen from the tire shop.
      We say the unsayable when we smash our palm meat against rubber,

or spin a tire on each finger. Sometimes we force a little of our own breath
      through the valve stem before we bottle it closed.
That kind of vintage. In the waiting room we bog our way past
      the customers to get water or coffee.

They flicker up from their magazines to eye these tar creatures
    the earth burped up. I am a blood-lamp lit when they do this.
I'll duck my head low and crawl to please you, Lord.
    Forgive me this backhoe in my chest

(I put the tires on that too) scooping too much fire
    from your bright body, but wanting to know you,
Lord, solid as a Cooper Cobra I can roll across the topmost curve
    of this earth.

I am porous, Father. I will drink you up.
    I'll big bang my skin at the tire shop.

These Nail Holes in Our Palms

October cold and I'm in the kitchen
pacing the oak floor with my hood up.
My sister's strapped to a bruised moon
and she's lifting a bottle of vodka to her mouth,
spitting at the heart of a continent. Colorado,
her Ed Mullen split in half by a train
even as she pinched her wedding dress,
held it before her like an awkward dance partner.
There's a train steaming on its haunches
along the first set of tracks, idling there
with those boxcars stretching behind it
like houses from his old neighborhood.
Eddie, you could have hit the snooze alarm,
coughed and rolled over, or gone 64 instead
of 65 mph. You could have gone jangling
back with your keys to kiss Lisa on the cheek
one more time and been the sixth or seventh car
in line instead of the fourth when that second iron pig
came squealing in the predawn dark.
I want a blacksmith's shop and forge,
the heat and clang of my hammer down on every vowel,
every consonant. I want to plant palm trees
to shade every skin wearer, starting with my sister;
to rend the sky down like some feeble circus tent.
I want to lay the backs of my hands to the ground
so live oaks and lemon trees sprout through
those nail holes we all have in our palms.

In the Truck's Back Draft

There's the purr of the road we love, your silk and my silk spilling in a trail behind us. You say we are books not kites and I wine to a rich hue of blue. You laugh and roll the windows down so our pages flutter like all manner of white birds inside our cruiser cab. Some of them ripping out the windows with our syllables on them, caught for a while in the truck's back draft and dragged along with us until they lose their flutter power and slide off into the ditch. You let go of the wheel because I hold on to too much and want to go back crawling in the ditch with you lining the high beams up so I can gather the lost pages. I want to say we crash into the corn and shred through it like our own children, but what happens is you roll the windows up and the bird spasms turn back into pages and flutter down to the floor to rest. I unclip the safety belt and place my mouth to where the heat is breaking around the neckline of your shirt. I test your ribs for breath then settle into your lap and rest there under the turning wheel, the light with its slippery fingers on our dashboard. More of the hum of this world and the hum of the wind inside your chest, a few stray pages still fluttering down on top of me.

Flesh

I'm writing the elms back home
about my dark-haired girl
whose spirit drenches the
blue sky and mud and fire
hydrant flesh I kiss. I'm sliding

my letter along a phone line
that arcs like some kite string
down through this divided
landscape. I'm pressing my lips
against yellow yellow leaves

and street sign skins, all shivering
her flesh where I'm kissing it.
I'm tearing her out of bricks
drenched with her firefly
essence. The bricks crumble,

they stale bread, they curbside
my street where I salt and eat her
to the traffic cop's whistle.
I drive to next and next city,
doing the same, tearing her skin

outside Rosa's Pizzeria—
where pinball machines wink
carnival lights inside my dark-haired girl,
her bread all bruised when I tear
another hunk from the cornerstone

at St. Clare of Montefalco,
where nuns play white soldier, and blow
their breath on all my altar boy smocks,

rocking them on their hangers
like little deflating children.

We will grow old
with the world, you and I,
and the earth will be our skeleton.

Movie Show

Julie and I act like little kids in private. We'll pause a movie
        and turn into slow-motion action figures in a film:
our faces melt or roar away at each other as we race
        to the bathroom, only one step every five seconds.
My mouth lets bloom an *Oh no*, as her fist
        comes hurtling through the air and ka-boom!

She rocks my jaw, teeth flying everywhere
        toward the promised land. I snatch her shirt
and halfback crash into her ribs, rock us
        both down on our bed. I gain the edge and crawl
on top. More slow-motion blows to the jaw,
        her face rocking left right left right left

on our pillow even after I stop hitting.
        Now I'm in the lead, scrambling over the lip
of the waterfall at the back of our bed. She mallets her
        fists down on my back so I flop to our shag carpet
like some big-time wrestler knocked senseless.
        She claws up my hair in both hands, smashes

my head over and over against the carpet.
        I let it bounce like a basketball after she's done
and gone crawling to her feet. I swipe a feeble
        hand at her foot to trip her, send her diving face
first into our bedroom wall. Julie pancake
        smashes like Wile E. Coyote against a rock wall.

She drools her way to the floor, heaps herself
        up like a woman who has just been shot,
laughter chugging out of our mouths
        like the steam of a choo-choo train.

On a Piece of Paper You Were About to Burn

How do you hold the dead
when they're hammered into a room
so flat you can pick your teeth

with one corner of the picture? When you were the one
at that moment aiming the cheap camera
wanting to fold her light

into a square locket of time.
You could see Noah's ark and the earth,
all the light in the world concentrated in her brown eyes.

The Dixie Chicks were playing "Cowboy Take Me Away,"
and that didn't hurt your cause.
But now that she's a crumb inside the earth,

the song punches little whispery nail holes
in the bottom of your boat
so the fountain sends its fine mist raining up.

You rock on the kitchen floor hugging your own legs,
weeping and kissing a face so tiny
you could cover it with a penny.

You repeat the same prayer to her over and over,
as if your heart were the governor on death's engine.
How could God smash a room flat into a photo

and do it over and over again?
She's standing in the doorway to your bedroom
in that apartment you came home to after your I do's.

Soon she'll peel off her shirt for bedtime
shivering even before you drive the needle into her arm.
You miss the bird's nest made of hair on your dresser,

the kissing and kissing her baby-bald head
when you were young and in love with as much
blood as rain pouring out of your shoes.

III

We're in the car rolling toward cancerland, trees arching over this back country road creating this long tunnel. We just passed the hospital where they first diagnosed I had cancer, then the cemetery beside it. I always hated that: tombstones spilling across this hillside right beside the hospital. I should lie on my back on a blanket beside my Johnny, sleep outside tonight under the stars. And I worry again and again about him losing me.

Thought at the Parting of These Waters

Morning and evening
like two sides of one hand.

All the prickly stars
with their beard set

upon us. Who sees through
these molecular clothes

to where the skeleton
paws at the air as if

climbing a ladder,
or swimming feebly upward?

The river hounds us
wet and white and swift,

conspires with the colt
kicking in our chest,

and even our toes
point toward death.

How precious to hunger for
morning and the tilt

of all things—lamp shades
by windows, cups

of warm milk, fire hydrants
all lilting toward her

when I rise and pour
across the earth to where

her heart stands like some factory
with sun in every window

slanting its legs
to press upon the ash.

The way her loveliness summons
me like some trumpet

made of blood jutting up
amid the last dandelions

and dying grass to sing to her.

Who Can Say

what sea waits inside us
    kneeling along some church pew,
or reclining on a bench tossing bread
    crumbs to the pigeons?

Sure the pews were once waves
    breaking upon that sea,
and sometimes the choirmaster
    flashes his arms behind the clouds,

or the oaks thrash in the yard
    conducting the leaves with the ghosts
and the flames and their whereabouts
    no one, not even death, can put out.

What other with her breath will set those pews
    collapsing against that sea,
hurtling all the kneelers with their prayers
    against God knows what altar?

               ×

We are lighter now, my love and I,
    folding the sky down
like a napkin and lacing it
    inside her handbag.

She has an appetite for the next step
    so we drift along the riverbank,
sweet with our slit-mouths and rags
    the dogwoods have stitched together.

Who can say what seed breaks open
    in our mouths when we kiss?
Or when we stop kissing,
    the fire draining from our loins

to spell such things in the grass.
 Beyond the forest and three rivers
ten thousand thousand lifeboats we set to drift
 brimming almost birdbath with water.

Sure the refractory sun
 shimmers in those pools
as we sit on a hillside amid the swaying grass
 with our foreheads touching.

Just like always the sunlight reaches with its fingers
 to take hold of us,
as if the wide earth were the cradle
 it was rocking us in.

Song for a Factory Girl

That ship of stone can have you
part of the time. There's a haul
of rubies in the hull
of the hull
behind your brown eyes.

Sure the tar sea rolls under you,
a timberline of forklifts
and telephone poles, men and women
with dirt-penny faces.

Jackhammer birds peck
along the surface of that sea,
but see how the stones warm to my touch?
Each cinder block
turns to warm bread
that fluffs in the oven
so the factory grows taller.

I'm the man with the music note face.
Harp strings hang from my shoulders
instead of arms. You are a map
made of blood with slices for eyes
and two mouths.

I sing the wine of you, the heart's shell
crushed under foot. Who would whisper this
mystery but the leaves or stones
folded with the ghosts:
One soul will emerge
from the thrashing crowd
who will change your life forever.

Go steady now with the lift and plunge
of that sea, there where you bow

with your acorn eyes
to stamp out the work.

Look to the ribbons
that flutter behind your legs.
When they shape-shift into chains,
I will warm them to some softness for you.
My fingers tremor at the door to you.

And so the great ship of stone
rises on its toy sea. Remember,
now that you are my home
your heart with its own fingers
can set aside the stones.

Tire Shop Poem Revisited

I've saved Sean Webber in the office for last,
fashioned for him a kind of chair carved out of heartwood
so he could take up residence there and begin to cook,
or be cooked from the inside out by love.
He's a rascal John Brown with his beard pitched
from his chin to his chest and quick to laugh.
Customers toss their light at the foot of his talk,
bring him venison sausage and cases of Budweiser
like aluminum bouquets. Once he rowed his boat
onto an ice floe, then rowed the floe to the center
of the lake to do some ice fishing.

You workers who only pour sweat into your labor
miss the soul of it: so many of our kinsmen
rip through their lives at high speeds with that silk
made of rubber we laced under them.
Sean and I were tire busters when some of these kids
were still in diapers. Someday I'll roll myself
in a wheelchair and lower the hoist,
snatch up the impact gun in my lap,
listen to the sweet clatter of lug nuts falling
into my beggar's cup
like shattered teeth that swirl around in a mouth
and then get spit out.

My own lass, when she was alive, used to bat her eyes
at Sean and toss some flakes of kindness into his beard.
He called her Jewels and she'd curtsy in her blood-skirt for him.

One night I roamed around all drunk until dawn.
I was with one of Sean's friends—a brawler
who took a shine to me. Sean made us coffee with the sun
coming up and I wrestled some puzzle pieces with his son,
then sluiced out of doors to chase a baseball across the sky—
home to where my Dame was sleeping.

Today there's a rare lull in the thunder shop.
Sean and I happen into a pocket of dirty light
by the door to bay one, there where no one else can hear.
He's telling me the inside story about his son,
who stole a car and crashed his whole life
into a field of trees. Facing hard time, he finds a plat,
a place where they plant new houses. Sean's son climbs
inside one of them. The boy finds a piece of pine to write on.
He leaves his mother's phone number for the police,
tells her he's sorry and that he loves her, then flings the rope
over the rafters, loops the rope around his neck,
slits his wrists and jumps.

"Dogger, we go to sleep every night
with that piece of wood in our bedroom."

You could sling that rope over a tree limb
in the next life, tie an old tire to it
so the boy could kick his legs
and swing in the yard, swing so high
he kicks every one of your stars, Lord,
kicks them right in the mouth.

I Have Cut Glass Blooming from My Chest

I've placed in the window where
it might catch light, the stained-glass hand
my wife made when she lived in this city
with its creaking stone ships
marooned all over the landscape.
The hand has three ruby rings on it,
and it's blooming from a glass earth,
straining to touch the ruby stars.

We have headlights and moonlight here,
rubies that flare inside the chests of passersby.
They ignite the rings on the fingers
in the window where the morning
light warms its blood through it.

Julie's cut-glass hand is punching back
into this world to lay siege
to the unreachable stars.

My lass practiced her flying as a girl:
she'd lunge from the staircase
and flap her arms over a pile of pillows,
believing, even as she crashed,
that if she trained hard enough
one day she would get there.

I posture toward the street,
plant her hand
in my chest to give it blood.

My lass plucks the stars
from the sky like cotton
so you'll remember the ways
you climbed as a child to where

you bent with the birches
and came parachuting to the earth
like a star of Bethlehem
too heavy for any tree
to hold you.

Quarter

I praise the quarter I find on the street where it pools and spreads so I go swimming inside silver. I have slid my quarter under a burning house so the house sinks into water and the fire hisses and pops. The books and mattresses all get sopping wet. Children swim to the windows with little bubbles rising from their mouths as the house drowns. I play scuba diver in my quarter swimming with the moonbeams to the children waving back to me, easy on their elbows near the window plucking their eyes at their new street. Their mother near the stove and she's flipping sodden pancakes. The funny way her hair floats up. Now the neighbors gather with their flashlights along the wet edges of my quarter. I can see among their beams the round lifesaver on a string cast over the water for us to swim our necks into. I am snapping slow rocks with my underwater slingshot to break the glass so the children can swim back up with me. I show them how to grip a fat beam falling from a fat flashlight, grip it ropelike so they can haul themselves up, their heads popping like champagne corks across the surface. When I swim down again, I find bits of glass around the edges of the window like shark's teeth jutting from the wood. I stick my neck in its mouth, and see a boy skipping steps up the staircase. I am swimming after him all breaststroke inside this house bubbling down into deeper waters. I tell him, chugging vowels into his ear, We'll dry the quarter out later so your house pops out of the earth like in a pop-up book. He won't have it. Now he's bubbling his mouth under his bed, and he's jabbing at my underwater skull with his underwater drumsticks. I pass his mother on the way out. I'm pointing up through the chimney I'll swim through since she already has the windows boarded up. I beckon to her, too, but she shakes her head no, I'm not leaving. She reaches to fold the T-shirts and blouses and blue jeans floating all about the room. Sometimes I hear the boy drumming inside my pocket, drumming his little sticks in George Washington's head.

A Mother Is a Living Blossom

My grandmother blew a perfect bubble
between her legs, then vanished six months later.
Barbed wire swaddled her baby Jesus,
even if my father couldn't feel it.
I have crept in to watch him sleep,
curled and sometimes wiggling,
with a sharpened hatchet
on the floor beside his bed.

Once in a jovial mood I went diving
headfirst between my wife's legs,
where I rubbed the crown of my head
as she giggled and squirmed.
With two fistfuls of my hair in her hands,
I kept saying, *I want to go home. I want to go home.*

My father is a clown's face, a painted man
now that my mother has gone
to her separate bedroom
in some cloudy corner of the house.
He slips out at night to bask
under that streetlamp on Somerset and Brunswick.

The words tumble like stones
from the pages of the book in his hands
until my father is left holding no story at all.
That blue light that pools beneath him
is where my father wants to rest,
even if its warmth is a paltry substitute
for the bloodbath his mother once gave him.

Some say a poem is an extravagant riddle,
puzzle pieces in a white box.
What is this shrapnel born out of the human spirit?
Sure it cools into what we call words,
but when the reader's eyes hit, it is reignited.

Mother, wrap my father in a blanket
of your own freckles.
Father, pick the roses carefully
from my mother's eyes. Remember:
you placed a typhoon on her ring finger.

I Watch Her Ride a Current Around the Deli

The body is fire and it's saying
 its language high and soundless.

It manifests as a force of nature,
 as if God could attach

a silencer to the wind, or teach a river
 to hush its warble over the rocks.

He sweeps a silencer over the barks
 and cries of birds,

gathers those cries cumulative,
 pours lightning cracks,

the rumblings of trains,
 and the hiss from every cannonball heart

into a sack that He lifts
 and offers to each of us

so we are rivers speaking to each other,
 wind languages, the music of whales

across the table when we glance
 up from the steaming earth and—

hold on to it now, love—
 just look at each other.

Monsieur Yeats

Yeats, if he's on
God's good side,
takes his stroll
past my bed

of coals each night,
jabbing at them over
and over with his cane,
as if he has lost something.

April 8, 2008

Earth, receive an honoured guest.
—W. H. Auden

I.

The nurses kept saying, Tell her it's okay to go.
A nectar of love bruised their bewildered faces
and I wanted to trick it into Julie's IV sack.
She had a burn mark big as a giant's hand along her neck.
I cupped my own hand around her bald head
and she breached back almost to consciousness, moaned
from so deep in her earth, a Julie sound and I devoured it.
Sometimes I'd say what the nurses asked me to say,
other times I'd whisper: *Don't leave me here.*

I wanted her body to be an earth
that went on and on forever.

II.

Winter held its tentacles to our eyes
as we watered my wife with dew those final fifty-two days.
A halo of the living surrounded her bed
as my son's tears anointed her forehead.

Now the weather was letting go of the stones
of cheekbones, the pretty perfumed faces.
Beyond the hospital, as we neared her petrifaction,
people sat sipping blood on bar patios
and everywhere along that anthill
citizens sliced the fleshy canvas.

III.

The godhead roaring in my chest
says there's no such thing as death.
I need only plant one crumb of my love behind her ribs
and her ruby heart will bloom forever.

I remember us both on a Friday night
deciding to use our hands as erasers
to erase the hospital and go on a date.
It was the end of a week in quarantine, more than a month in,
and we prepared Julie for her first outing.
The nurses fawned over her for forty-five minutes,
new diapers and clean linen in her lap,
my lass thanking them every time they brushed one feather
across the air for her.

She beamed through her bruised skin
the kind of stoicism a mountain might have
if a mountain could swaddle itself in flesh
and house a fat pear of light stolen from the sun.

She stood for that first dance, one arm about my waist,
one wrist dangling over my shoulder as I backpedaled
for those first baby steps toward the door.
Her legs had atrophied to noodles.

In the hallway she spread her arms as we shoved off
in the wheelchair, her smile crinkling the mask
over her nose and mouth. "I'm in a ragtop convertible
with the top down and the wind is in my hair."

Round and round the hospital hallway park on our promenade,
tipping our hats congenially to the other passengers in the gallows,

with their rosy partners strolling beside them,
as if the wind would never come to eat each one of them alive.

I was stuffed to the seams with grace
until Julie finally shooed me away and I vanished
into the coal night, trying not to flare brighter
than any star in the firmament.
I took those small steps away from the city of light.

Where goes this water from my eyes
in the remembering?
Does it strike my love's eyes in the earth
and make them dazzle?

IV.

It's the morphine, Dude. I keep seeing things that aren't there.
Yesterday there was a river of blood rushing in the hallway.
The nurses and doctors were all laughing.
Then a marching band came splashing through it.
It was my high school marching band and I was playing flute.

From the tiny porthole in the corner of her room
sunlight pours as from some chalice
over the right side of Julie's face.

Last night patients were floating into the sky like great balloons.
Look, two little girls are playing in the lake at the foot of the bed.
I know they're not there but I see them.

I aim my eyes with her eyes and watch those girls squat
with their knees up around their faces

scooping sand into a pail.
My hands are magic wands
with the light gone out of them.
We're cheek against cheek in her bed
when she points her nose toward the window.

See, now there's a ten-story Martell outside the hospital
and he's wearing his football uniform.
He's got his helmet under one arm
and he's smiling in at us.

I can see him out there, our son,
a tower of a boy standing guard over my lass.

The worst part is at night.
I feel your warmth right next to me.
Then I roll over to put my arms around you and you're gone.
Out into the night, I think.
My wild man's roaming the earth like he does.
Then I remember where I am, take hold of my pillow
and whisper to it, "Oh, Dude."

Why couldn't her body be an earth
that went on and on forever?

V.

A few days before she died, in that torture chamber
with the pretty painted walls and kindly nurses,
I thought to ask for some narcotic
that would coax me back from the edge,
the mania was broiling in me that loud.

I bolted from the hospital and ran weeping
through the city of Ann Arbor, chanting to her Virgin Mary,
"Mary, Mother of God, please reach down
and take her up into your arms," until lost and fuming breathless
I punched to the end of a street where a silver stone cathedral
loomed before me and I ran up the church steps spreading my arms
to the large wooden doors, laying my cheek against them
begging the church and the sky and Julie's Mary over and over,
"Mother of God, please reach down and take her up into your arms."
I wanted her to cup her palm around that room
and lift it like a burning apple into the heavens.

VI.

Her breath kept pouring out against my neck.
I could not make it stop. Her breath kept pouring out,
I tell you. Yet her pink face beamed swollen with hope
as we ushered in the next and next and next sentence.

We were looping the loops of our stories into a rope
made of tawny light spawning deeper and deeper
into the mystery of two are better than one
until I became the only thread matriculating forward into the dirty sky

like some lost dolphin swimming in that cosmic sea without her.
My cry reached from the bottom of God to the crown of nowhere.
My nerves were the tips of barbed-wire prongs
spooling outside factories and prisons all over the world.

The body is a volition engine and dies hard.
Fifteen seconds after she passed I squeezed a last gasp
from her and dropped her onto the bed,
like I'd done something wrong.

When they zipped her into the body bag,
I tore the hospital's walls and the circus tent
where we hand over our dead
for the ride into the bowels of that place.

VII.

How do you go on living when you've died,
incremental over time until the final carnage
asks your ashes to play Hercules?

When I was a boy, Greg Grillo the hockey stud
ripped round and round the block on a summer night
until he became a helicopter prop
lifting the whole neighborhood skyward—
power and unearthly eloquence and steam.

All of us kids would drop our basketballs
and peashooters and stuff marbles back into our pockets
as we were pulled magnetically
toward this animal scarcely sparking
his frictionless feet against the earth.

His father barked at Greg with each pass
and held the stopwatch like a pitted heart.
Between the jingle of his keys when he got home from work
and the tin slam of his front door
all you ever bumped into with Mr. Grillo
was the armor-coated man, the abrasive exterior.

Until one night, in a city of more than a million,
amid the magnified stillness that happens
when everyone in the world falls down,

I heard a mournful melody wrap the houses
and mount the tunnel of elms along our street.
I crawled in my pj's to my bedroom window
and found, in nothing but his underwear,
Mr. Grillo cradling a saxophone, tottering drunk
like a blade of grass in high winds and licking
the bricks and the walls behind the eyes and the cloudless night
with this language like a living sea breaking from his chest.
He lifted a colossal sadness to that horn,
and when he blew he filled the heavens with his cry.

I Saw a Whiskey Bottle Turn into a Drop of Rain

There's a river of light inside my lass
    and I'm hauling it out of her

veins like rope.
    Even if she's in the dirt.

I saw my love's shadow with a strawberry
    heart pinned to its chest;

needles there too
    drilling at her brown eyes.

I saw meteorites banging their fists
    into the ground around her grave.

I saw my wife warm her blood-engine
    and rise from the earth

shaking off the dirt crumbs
    so she could come home to me.

IV

Dude, if you're reading this and I'm gone, you are my world.

If

If I could tie a river around my love's waist like ribbon,
    make sails out of her blood
and pin down death like a squirming bug.

If I could lift and rock each coffin in my arms
    I would start with hers.

Driving Through the Field of Hearts

I reached out the window
    to grab even one stalk

slapping at the front grille,
    or getting smashed below us.

The roots kept coming up,
    plant after plant, like I was

unstitching the field. I kept my arm
    out there for miles,

breezy and straining to hold on
    to that aurora borealis of red blossoms.

                    ✶

Was it the field being lifted
    and planted in the sky,

or the eight stories of stairs I climbed
    to where some hand was

shaping itself around her hospital bed
    and lifting it into heaven?

I don't mean figurative light pouring
    over the edges of that palm:

I-beam girders and gut wiring reduced to feathers;
    nurses circling under that tree of life

where the twenty-one IV sacks
    hung ripe as fruit.

I didn't have that rag of shame in my chest
        as I left what we in the world call stairs,

cut past her name tag on the door
        sifting through such blinding rays

pouring from her face.
        I reached one more time to kiss

the bruise circles around her eyes,
        kiss and kiss her baby-bald head.

                    ✳

But then this field of hearts
        where my love began to manifest

on the backseat. I started twirling that jump rope
        and even the soft plumage in our chests

lunged and settled each time the vine
        made another pass.

My lass wasn't one more dry root in the earth,
        though she seemed unimpressed

with that arm made of mist
        holding the rope on the other side.

I could see a hunk of our bedroom
        mirror hanging from her neck.

It was shedding red blossoms
        all over our bedroom floor.

There'd be enough to fill our pillows.
    Enough to cover her up to her throat

in hearts when she cried from our bedroom,
    Dude, will you come tuck me in?

We Were All of Us There

Reading the flutter of eyelashes.
    Trading our own teeth

so we could sing better.
    We were all there pouring mud

into the cannon's blue mouth.
    We came with the sea stuffed in our pockets.

We were sweeping falling glass
    and lost languages,

using butterflies instead of words
    to speak to each other.

Daily This Leaf Blown

like a perfect palm over my mouth.
Forces like gale winds with flying glass

and all of them swirling awful around the spine.
How to hawk my arms over this

piano and let fall from every talon
drops that will tap at the keys for me

that I might affix no more than the rain's name
to a poem, or say the tendril tips of leaves,

the branches of a tree composed it?
I'll smear my lips with lipstick, then kiss the page,

leave that hoofprint as my mark,
or claim it's the boy on the cross

with his feet dunked in ink
who uncorks the nails and goes tramping

over the skin of this lake
where I sometimes whirl like a dancer

across the surface of this canvas,
looping and tracing indelible in flame

a thing everlasting.

While My Body Lasts

I want to crawl inside St. Clare of Montefalco
and write my poems by candlelight.
I can hide under the pews

when the dust sweepers come
to sweep up all that fall-away skin
that flakes off the living and the dead.

I have a scraped-up silver lighter
to spark the votive candles
if I need them to keep me warm.

No need to don my old altar boy smock.
The stained-glass towers and vault
ceiling always were a kindly blanket

draped over my boy shoulders.
I'll pace and practice my sermon,
then bow and carve the sounds

into that cave wall. I'll pitch my arms
like some hawk's so the ashes slide off
like snow. We all remember

how warm she once was.
My lass was the great moth of love
and when she finally came,

between her body and the wall
I felt almost sealed up inside
a great boat of blood again.

When my love was still alive
I could fling myself through vast cathedrals:
my first shedding, the bricks from that city

where I taught blackbirds to sing
great earthen hymns through their fingers;
the second shedding, one of silos

and green seas and flocks of untamable birds
ripping from the earth the way an alphabet might
rupture skyward in defiance of all poetry.

I return at last and my chest is stuffed
with hay bales, horses, and houses
where I've heard you can find needles

stabbed into the wall like darts.
I return at last in a swoop over that hill
where the dogs might be dragging her

arm out by its root. When she sees it's me
in the distance, she spreads her arms,
that speck as I approach growing

to lovely rag doll, then woman, sweet flesh
of my flesh. Even the steam of her breath
under the neckline of my shirt comes pouring

its benediction of human warmth.
The candles and the church
don't matter much now, do they,

though many a birthday cake has been lit
with our wishes and we lay those wishes
inside the earth.

This Noise from My Fingers

It astounds me the ways
I scale the sky. Every day I have to
relearn my body.

Who will tell us to the world?
Our children whose heads we breathe into
like seashells casting those spells

our mothers once wooed us with?
A playground where we became the mist
hanging over everything?

We knew it was our insides
tugged inside out at last.
Once when I was a boy on the dodge

hopping fences, I let my leg hang over the lip
to that other world. I stopped
on top of that wobbly fence,

and hit the pause button on the world.
I held it all: the shadows from the plum tree
whose fruit we used to peg cars with;

the dust from my father's broom;
even the boys chasing after me.
I knew the time was passing

and took even the shadows of the branches
into those pockets God had sewn
into my body for the traveling.

I kissed the moment flush
on the mouth, then let it go,
surrendered again to the earth

with silencers on my tennis shoes.
Maybe time itself came brushing
the trail behind me until it vanished

clean off the grass, and I took up residence
with all the other balloons
floating along the landscape.

Serenade for a Word Crew at a Last Chance High School

Someday I'll be done and I'll rest,
let the dandelions sprout right out
of my chest. The flesh of the flesh
ain't no bulletproof vest.
I bury thunder in the mines,
got wind chimes and rhythm and rhymes
hanging from the vines under my eyes.
I use silk to wrap a thug up,
turn hands into handcuffs,
blow white powder off the rooftops.
Where I teach in the D,
kids got sacred fires
tucked under their sleeves.
We get down to it, roll sounds 'n' syllables
up and smoke our way right through 'em.
My kids go home to that brick school
where being a warrior's the game,
or a player, or a white-boy hater.
I'm here to save the fire they're made of.
I'm a crusader, a whodunnit nowhere player
rolling crack houses like dice along alleyways,
and I'm saying these kids are living flames.
They go bold in their armor,
but that armor is what I want to slaughter.
Polish up that red rock in their chests,
rock-a-bye the whole city
in my arms while they rest.

On My Porch Steps

for Matt Cashen

Tonight none of my oceans
are tearing their white hands.
You and I are floating
in a shotgun shell

that emptied its powder
into night. The live oaks
on the hill behind us shake
loose their camouflage,

slip their roots from under-
ground to follow us.
I climb over piled alphabets
my angels hammer into spark,

climb over rainwater, the rose
bushes, the ghost branches
of Dutch elms. I haul my way past
electric lines that link

their wiring from star to star,
until there's only one ladder
left balancing one leg
on either side of a roof peak

and it's jutting its bones
into the stars. (Still the smell
from the fresh-tilled fields,
miasma from the wetlands ponds.)

I hang from the highest rung,
pendulum my legs under
the ladder, and release.
Now I'm latching one

fist then another around
stray leaves from last winter
and chimney ashes gusting up.
I can't drop my hands into your earth,

can't say I know the way by leaps
and bounds toward a happiness
that's simple as bread rising.
But kick the ladder down

when you reach the highest rung
and lunge up after me, brother.
I'm leaving feathers there that will
bear you off, set you swinging

from feather to fiery stone,
into your own great unknown.

Dearest Flaming Crumbs in Your Beard, Lord

May my body last, so I can sing apple blossoms
blown out of my open mouth and raining their petals
onto ragtop convertibles and fields of wild asparagus;
raining their petals onto milk barns and silos and
blowing them wide open; petals melting down
onto the tongues of men and women
hanging their clock faces out every open window
along Sixth Avenue; wild blossoms gusting into doorways
and tumbling up staircases; blossoms whirlwinding
around the bare ankles, around the heart of my beloved
and climbing with her into bed;
blossoms swirling into hospital rooms
and churches and spilling their feathers
onto the shimmering outlines of just gone people
down on their knees—those feathery vowels,
those blood-drop men and women locking their fingers
around the lowest rung of those ladders we haul around
like crosses mounted to our backs;
ladders jutting their bones into the stars;
sweet ladders we'll one day climb, pushing our faces
through the blue womb of this world into that garden
of stars bell-knocking on their vines.

The Deft Touch of Angels

Can you see my love outside,
a pink and white swan there
on the moonless side of our cottage?

There's a roselike flame
rising from the earth where she stands.
When I reach for her the tips

of my fingers go drowning in it,
press through the flames to touch
the little blood-house she lives in.

She's weeping inside a barn
that's held underwater, the roses spawning up
so they brushstroke and burn.

If I had the proper arms, say,
the deft touch of angels, I'd tend her from above,
make one flag from the rag flames

moving through her, run that flag
up every pole, flutter it over the nations.
The red bird in my chest

keeps repeating, You're just a man,
just a man who wants to push
the tombstones away and live,

to eat your oats and run long miles
until the beasts lie down in your blood
to chew a blade of grass and rest.

I will row with my breath and greet her
in that country, rub another sunset over her skin,
sit across from her on our porch,

two elementals with our morning coffee,
a slender stick of lightning
in each of our hands.

I Flew Out to You Through Bone Timber

through ash and want for your pink skin
to flame again inside the earth. I rose under
Bible passages ripping through the pages, arching like a dolphin,
no, a shriveled locket of time.
We rose each day like flaming birds
dusting the embers off our sheets. We traded for kindness
steaming in a mug and coughed our morning words
that fell like snowflakes at our feet.
My sweet locket of time, there's no birdbath where we flicker
our wings, no offering of blood or dew.
All the birds do is bicker
over the living wine in you.
Disassemble this flesh to morning dew
so I can seep into the earth and come home to you.

Seal Up All in Rest

The heart blown up so many times
the skin hates the bones

for forcing it to stand,
for not letting the flesh just fall

steaming to the earth.
Let me lie down now on the grass

and empty out, Lord. Let my heart rest
under one leaf pressing

like my love's hand once did.
I am too tired for translation.

Take away my bones, Lord.
Let my skin fall

through the bedsprings,
through the floorboards.

I'll make so small a splash
against the sweet grass.

I'm Only Sleeping

Another six-pack in the tub
floating downstream
next to my bed.

I fall asleep with the light on
and a beer in hand. It tips over
so I wake up in what

feels like my own piss.
My Jack Russell Sparky's drowsing
two feet higher at the foot of the bed.

He's there with all those clothes heaped up
and layered over Julie's hospital things:
her bathrobe, diapers, and soft bottoms;

lotion for rubbing her face and bald head.
Let go now, Johnny.
The moon is writing

sweeter sentences on the water
than you anyway.
Pull the earth over you now and sleep.

Acknowledgments

The author would like to thank the following souls: Russell Thorburn and Matt Cashen for the indelible imprint they left on these poems; the Moulds clan, especially Angie and Dave: you gave me the finest woman on earth to love, and still wrap me in a cloth of goodness; Judy Estes, NP, and Dr. Kaminsky, who embraced my wife every time he gave her good news; Denny Hayes for lodging and the fellowship of family when I needed it most, and to Francie Skarett for always being there.

For the first nurse, my mother, who taught me tenderness is the most powerful medicine.

Blessings to those guardian angels who helped keep me alive after and who still sustain me: Karen and Steve Goebel, Susie Boudeman, Fred Guthrie, Susan Ramsey, Eric Frie, Dawn and Jim Reeves, Tana Harding and Cheryl Bowers, Bill Palmer, Philip Levine, Stuart Dybek, Shirley Clay Scott, and the whole Hosler, Smith, and Iott clans.

Widest thanks to the following for their timely support during the writing of this book: the Academy of American Poets; PEN American Center; the Carnegie Fund for Authors; Peter and Barbra Parish; Dr. Smith, DDS; Hank Meijer and Leisel Litzenburger; Bonnie Jo Campbell; and everyone who helped support our bone marrow transplant fund-raiser.

I owe such a debt, the debt of life and hope, to Emily Smith and the staff at Lookout Books, especially Ben George, whose life is indeed holy.

Publication Notes

Alaska Quarterly Review: "The Deft Touch of Angels" and "Quarter"

American Poetry Review: "I'm Old Enough to Be My Own Father"

Bomb: "I Straddle the Earth"

Ecotone: "April 8, 2008," "I'm Only Sleeping," "I Saw a Whiskey Bottle Turn into a Drop of Rain," "Seal Up All in Rest," "This Noise from My Fingers," "We Were All of Us There," "Who Can Say," and "Why Everything Is a Poem"

Failbetter: "Near the Old Packard Plant" and "Night and Its Strange Likeness to a Diego Rivera Mural"

Iowa Review: "I Watch Her Ride a Current Around the Deli" and "Monsieur Yeats"

North American Review: "These Nail Holes in Our Palms"

Paris Review Daily: "Tender Range"

Ploughshares: "On a Piece of Paper You Were About to Burn" and "We Dance on a Spinning Log"

Poetry: "If" and "Thought at the Parting of These Waters"

taint: "Flesh"

Third Coast: "I Flew Out to You Through Bone Timber"

Vincent Brothers Review: "On My Porch Steps"

The poems "Dearest Flaming Crumbs in Your Beard, Lord," "Flesh," and "On My Porch Steps" previously appeared in the chapbook *Yellow-Haired Girl with Spider*.

The poem "I'm Only Sleeping" was reprinted in *The Pushcart Prize XXXVI*.

Lookout Books

Lookout is more than a name—it's our
publishing philosophy. Founded as the
literary book imprint of the Department of
Creative Writing at the University of North
Carolina Wilmington, Lookout pledges to seek
out works by emerging and historically under-
represented voices, as well as overlooked gems
by established writers. In a publishing landscape
increasingly indifferent to literary innovation,
Lookout offers a haven for books that matter.

Text Goudy Old Style 10.2 / 13.2
Display Goudy Old Style Italic 14